Choral Reading
Grades 2-3
Table of Contents

Part One: Introduction
Introduction. 2
Features. 3
Suggestions for
Supplementary Activities. 4
Suggested Props 5
Use. 6
Parent Letter 7
Student Certificate. 8

Part Two: Choral Reading Selections

Theme 1: Rhymes from Around the World
Kye Kye Kule 9
Chocolate Rhyme. 10
Hukilau 13
Frere Jacques 15
Today Is Monday 17

Theme 2: What's to Celebrate?
Thanksgiving Day. 19
I Saw Three Ships. 21
We Shall Overcome 23
Happy Valentine's Day. 25
Washington and Lincoln 27
Michael Finnegan 29
Chinese New Year 31

Theme 3: That's the Silliest Thing!
If All the World Were Paper 33
Two Silly Ladies 35
Calico Pie 37
Have You Ever Seen?. 39
Betty Botter 41

Theme 4: Sun, Wind, and More
Weather Medley 43
A Calendar. 45
The Wind 47
Autumn Fires 49
Snowy Day. 51

Theme 5: Plants and Animals Alive and Well
The Green Grass Grew All Around . . . 53
Over in the Meadow 56
Animal Fair 59
The Leopard. 61
The Squirrel 63
Skylark 65

Theme 6: Our Colorful World
What Is Pink?. 67
If. 69
The Star 71
The Land of Nod 73
My Shadow 75
The Swing 77
Turtle Soup 79
Ravioli 81
Manners Medley 83
Hurt No Living Thing 85

Theme 7: Tales that Teach a Lesson
The Gingerbread Man 87
Clever Girl 89
Belling the Cat. 91
King Midas. 93
The Crow and the Jug 95

What is choral reading?

Choral reading is a group reading experience designed to foster oral reading skills and promote excitement for reading. Students interact with a variety of texts, each piece carefully selected for its rhythm and rhyme or other appealing qualities for both reader and listener.

In choral reading, students read an assigned part, primarily in unison with a group. A few selections feature solo parts for dramatic emphasis. As the selection is read, students practice word recognition, expand reading vocabulary, and increase comprehension skills. As students read the poems and tales in this book, they develop expressive reading as they encounter musical language. After reading, the students are encouraged to relate what they have read to their own lives and interests.

Choral reading experiences build readers' confidence by putting them with a community of readers. Choral reading encourages readers to attempt to read in a positive learning environment. With a group, students practice reading with fluency and expression in a way that allows immediate success. Students develop their reading skills through the choral reading, and they apply these skills to new reading material.

By providing choral reading experiences, teachers can add a fresh, exciting element to reading instruction and allow students to read through participation.

Themes

This collection of choral reading selections is designed to pique students' interest in participation. The poems, songs, and stories are correlated to seven exciting themes:

- **Rhymes from Around the World**
  To present a multicultural perspective, selections in this theme feature traditional songs and rhymes from different cultures.

- **What's to Celebrate?**
  To focus on traditional holidays, these poems explore the reasons for the special day or provide verse traditionally shared for the celebration.

- **That's the Silliest Thing!**
  Perfect any time, these amusing selections entertain students and encourage them to be expressive.

- **Sun, Wind, and More**
  To explore the different types of weather and seasonal changes, these poems celebrate the natural world.

- **Plants and Animals Alive and Well**
  A perennial favorite of students, poems about flora and fauna can boost content area studies by encouraging students to observe and reflect upon nature.

- **Our Colorful World**
  This theme explores beauty in the world, as well as favorite activities of children.

- **Tales that Teach a Lesson**
  Stories from Aesop and other traditional tales that feature a moral for students to consider and apply to their own lives.

Features

A diverse selection of poems, rhymes, and stories build excitement and draw the reader in. Selections are arranged in thematic units and range from a multicultural perspective to traditional verses and tales to new works.

Many well-known poets are featured. The selections also draw on folk and traditional sources.

A variety of groupings is suggested for dramatic emphasis.

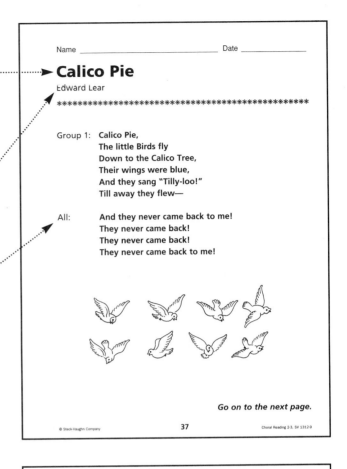

Name _____ Date _____

Calico Pie
Edward Lear
****

Group 1: Calico Pie,
The little Birds fly
Down to the Calico Tree,
Their wings were blue,
And they sang "Tilly-loo!"
Till away they flew—

All: And they never came back to me!
They never came back!
They never came back!
They never came back to me!

Go on to the next page.

© Steck-Vaughn Company   37   Choral Reading 2-3, SV 1312-9

Readers build fluency with texts that feature elements such as rhyme, rhythm, and repetition—perfect for oral reading.

Reading with a group fosters cooperation skills.

Each selection ends with a fun activity suggestion for extension to be completed independently or with a partner.

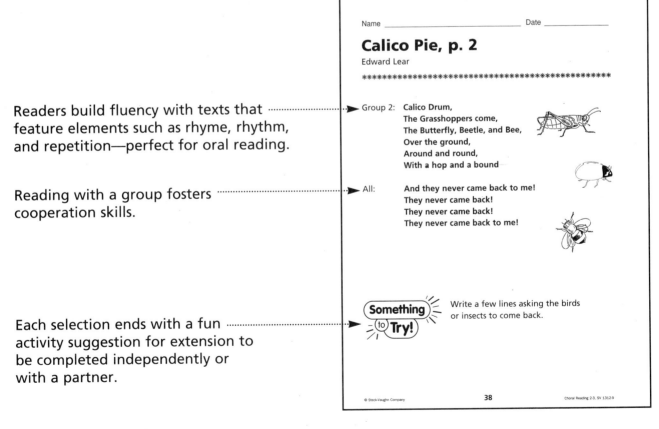

Name _____ Date _____

Calico Pie, p. 2
Edward Lear
****

Group 2: Calico Drum,
The Grasshoppers come,
The Butterfly, Beetle, and Bee,
Over the ground,
Around and round,
With a hop and a bound—

All: And they never came back to me!
They never came back!
They never came back!
They never came back to me!

Something to Try! Write a few lines asking the birds or insects to come back.

© Steck-Vaughn Company   38   Choral Reading 2-3, SV 1312-9

Suggestions for Supplementary Activities

1. Students can divide into groups, assign parts, and make costumes and props for a favorite choral reading. Then each group can perform the choral reading in front of the rest of the class. This is a fun way to interpret the choral reading and enable the students to bring it to life.

2. Have children create a poster to advertise their favorite choral reading. The students can share information about their favorite choral reading with the rest of the class.

3. Continue to spark the students' interest by inviting them to find other poems, stories, and articles relating to a theme. They can share the information and literature they find with the class.

4. Encourage students to write their own choral reading. Students can choose to write about something that really happened, or they can be creative and make it up. After choosing a topic, they can model their choral reading after one they have read and enjoyed.

5. Students can be assigned choral readings for homework to be read with older siblings or parents.

6. Have your students perform their favorite choral reading from the multicultural theme for other classes. They can use costumes or musical instruments to perform the choral reading. Then they can tell the other classes about the culture or tradition.

7. The students can write another stanza or verse for a choral reading. This will help them to focus on the rhythm, rhyme, and line structure of the choral reading.

8. Have the students depict their favorite choral reading by making a diorama. They can use paper, shoe boxes, and other art supplies to create a scene or their favorite part from the choral reading. Then have the students write a few sentences telling about the diorama.

9. If older students or classroom helpers visit your classroom, get them involved. Have visitors and students buddy-up to read the choral readings.

10. Allow your students to be creative by replacing a character in a choral reading that teaches a lesson with themselves. They can rewrite the choral reading to include things that have happened to them. This enables the students to give the choral reading meaning in their own lives.

11. Take your class to a local theater production that incorporates the use of choral reading. They will see how their daily activity is used and enjoyed in their community.

12. Record your class as they do a choral reading, and put the tape in a listening center for them to read along with and enjoy. Practicing their reading with the tape reinforces reading strategies and skills.

Suggested Props

The students can use props to make sound effects, to keep rhythm, and to act out the choral readings. This list is suggested to help save you time and facilitate prop-gathering.

Choral Reading Title	Possible Props
Kye Kye Kule	rhythm sticks
Chocolate Rhyme	mixing bowl, wooden spoons
Hukilau	fishing nets, fishing poles, fish, grass skirts, flower leis
Frere Jacques	pillows, bells
Today Is Monday	wash baskets, towels, cans of soup, beans
Thanksgiving Day	chairs arranged like a sled, coats, blankets
I Saw Three Ships	whistle, violin, three ships, dancing
We Shall Overcome	rhythm sticks, drum, tambourine
Happy Valentine's Day	large valentine cards, hearts
Washington and Lincoln	top hat, ax, American flag
Michael Finnegan	beards, fishing poles
Chinese New Year	dragons, candles, poppers and noisemakers
If All the World Were Paper	paper confetti
Two Silly Ladies	chair, ball, pail, net, pickle, flower, pin, thread, harp
Calico Pie	birds, bees, grasshopper, butterfly, beetle, drum
Have You Ever Seen?	sheet, hammer, needle, garden hose, clock, rake
Betty Botter	mixing bowl, spoon
Weather Medley	umbrellas
A Calendar	calendar
The Wind	kites, fans
Autumn Fires	big paper leaves, tissue paper flames
Snowy Day	snowflakes, coats, scarves
The Green Grass Grew All Around	paper grass, tree, bird's nest
Over in the Meadow	animals
Animal Fair	elephant, monkey
The Leopard	leopard, spots
The Squirrel	pecans, acorns, squirrel
Skylark	bird, nest, whistle, rhythm sticks
What Is Pink?	colors, rose, clouds, flower, swan, pear, grass, orange
If	ax, tree, lumberjack
The Star	stars, Moon, flashlights
The Land of Nod	drum, rhythm sticks, pillows, blankets
My Shadow	overhead projector, flashlights
The Swing	swing
Turtle Soup	soup can, bowl, spoon
Ravioli	shirt, jeans, shoe
Manners Medley	rhythm sticks, drum, shakers, tambourines
Hurt No Living Thing	insects
The Gingerbread Man	large gingerbread man, wooden spoon, fox, children
Clever Girl	king, daughter, cup, stone
Belling the Cat	cat, mice, bell necklace
King Midas	king, gold coins, princess
The Crow and the Jug	jug, pebbles, crow

Use

Select choral readings to correlate with a season, celebration, or unit of study.

↓

Duplicate and distribute the selection. Read through the entire selection with students.

↓

Discuss the content of the selection—the mood, message, and choice of words.

↓

Assign parts. You may wish to have students use a highlighting marker to indicate their parts on their copy.

↓

Provide time for students to read through their parts. Encourage students to ask for assistance as needed.

↓

Conduct the choral reading, encouraging students to use intonation, expression, and emphasis for a dramatic result. You may wish to repeat the reading several times. In some instances, you may even wish to have students reverse roles.

↓

Arrange for students to present some of their choral readings to an audience. Parent visitation days, parent-teacher meetings, or school assemblies are some occasions to entertain with choral readings. You might also consider having children practice on bus rides and perform on field trips.

Dear Family Members:

Our class will take off on a great reading adventure with choral reading. What is choral reading? It is a group reading with assigned parts. These experiences help develop a variety of reading skills. Students explore poetry and traditional stories. They practice reading with expression. They build confidence with oral reading and performing in front of an audience.

From time to time, your child may come home with a part to practice at home. You can help your child in the following ways:

- Encourage your child to read through the piece on his or her own, but provide help with any words that are difficult for your child.
- When your child is ready, listen to him or her read aloud. Be a great audience! Praise your child's efforts. Make only a few suggestions for improvement, if needed.

There will be opportunities for you to listen to your child participate in a choral reading. Look for an invitation soon!

Cordially,

CONGRATULATIONS!

This is to certify that

_____

is a **great** choral reader.

The reader's **favorite** selection is

_____

Name _____   Date _____

Kye Kye Kule (Chay Chay Koo-lay)

A Call-and-Response Song from Ghana, Africa

✳✳✳

Group 1: **Kye kye kule.** (Chay chay koo-lay)
(Put hands on your head.)

Group 2: **Kye kye kule.** (Chay chay koo-lay)
(Put hands on your head.)

Group 1: **Kye ko-fi nea.** (Chay koe-fee nea)
(Put hands on your shoulders.)

Group 2: **Kye ko-fi nea.** (Chay koe-fee nea)
(Put hands on your shoulders.)

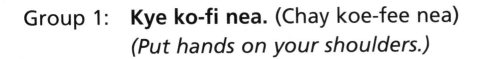

Group 1: **Ko-fi sa langa.** (Koe-fee sa lahn'-ga)
(Put hands on your waist.)

Group 2: **Ko-fi sa langa.** (Koe-fee sa lahn'-ga)
(Put hands on your waist.)

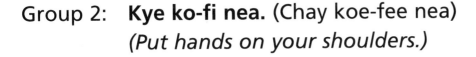

Group 1: **Ketaki langa.** (Kay-tay-chee lahn'-ga)
(Put hands on your knees.)

Group 2: **Ketaki langa.** (Kay-tay-chee lahn'-ga)
(Put hands on your knees.)

Go on to the next page.

Choral Reading 2-3, SV 1312-9

Name _____   Date _____

Kye Kye Kule, p. 2

A Call-and-Response Song from Ghana, Africa

****

Group 1:   **Kum adende.** (Koom a-dayn-day)
(Put hands on your ankles.)

Group 2:   **Kum adende.** (Koom a-dayn-day)
(Put hands on your ankles.)

Group 1:   **Kum adende. Hey!** (Koom a-dayn-day)
(Put hands on your ankles.)

Group 2:   **Kum adende. Hey!** (Koom a-dayn-day)
(Put hands on your ankles.)

All: **Hands on your head.**
           Hands on your shoulders.
           Hands on your waist.
           Hands on your knees.
           Hands on your ankles. Hey!

Sing and do the English version of this song, "Head and Shoulders, Knees and Toes."

10

Chocolate Rhyme

A Traditional Rhyme from Latin America

✱✱

Group 1: **Uno, dos, tres, cho-** (oono, dohs, thres, choe)
(Count with fingers.)

Uno, dos, tres, -co- (oono, dohs, thres, koe)
(Count with fingers.)

Uno, dos, tres, -la- (oono, dohs, thres, la)
(Count with fingers.)

Uno, dos, tres, -te (oono, dohs, thres, tay)
(Count with fingers.)

Bate, bate chocolate! (ba-tay, ba-tay choe-koe-la-tay)
(Rub palms together back and forth, as if using a chocolate beater.)

Go on to the next page.

Chocolate Rhyme, p. 2

A Traditional Rhyme from Latin America

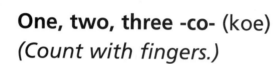

Group 2:   **One, two, three cho-** (choe)
(Count with fingers.)

One, two, three -co- (koe)
(Count with fingers.)

One, two, three, -la- (la)
(Count with fingers.)

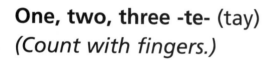

One, two, three -te- (tay)
(Count with fingers.)

Stir, stir the chocolate! (choe-koe-la-tay)
*(Rub palms together back and forth, as if using
a chocolate beater.)*

Make hot chocolate to share with
classmates or an audience.

Name _____   Date _____

Hukilau (Hoo-kee-lou)

A Traditional Song from Hawaii

✳✳✳✳✳✳✳✳✳✳✳✳✳✳✳✳✳✳✳✳✳✳✳✳✳✳✳✳✳✳✳✳✳✳✳✳✳✳

Group 1:   Oh we're going to the Hukilau.
Huki Huki Huki Huki Hukilau!
Everybody loves the Hukilau
With the lau lau and the kau kau
at the big luau.
We throw all our nets out into the sea
And all the ama ama come swimming to me.

Group 2:   Oh we're going to the Hukilau.
Huki Huki Huki Huki Hukilau!
What a wonderful day for fishing
The old Hawaiian way!
The Hukilau nets are swishing
Down on old Laie Bay.

Go on to the next page.

       Choral Reading 2-3, SV 1312-9

Hukilau, p. 2

A Traditional Song from Hawaii

****

All:

Oh we're going to the Hukilau.
Huki Huki Huki Huki Hukilau!
Everybody loves the Hukilau
With the lau lau and the kau kau
at the big luau.
We throw all our nets out into the sea
And all the ama ama come swimming to me.
Oh we're going to the Hukilau.
Huki Huki Huki Huki Hukilau!

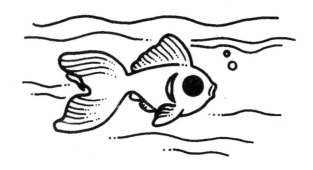

Read more about Hawaiian traditions.

Frere Jacques

A Traditional Song from France

****

Group 1:   **Frere Jacques,**

Group 2:   **Frere Jacques,**

Group 1:   **Dormez-vous?**

Group 2:   **Dormez-vous?**

Group 1:   **Sonnez les matines,**

Group 2:   **Sonnez les matines.**

Group 1:   **Din, din, don!**

Group 2:   **Din, din, don!**

Go on to the next page.

Frere Jacques, p. 2

A Traditional Song from France

****

Group 2: **Are you sleeping?**

Group 1: **Are you sleeping?**

Group 2: **Brother John!**

Group 1: **Brother John!**

Group 2: **Morning bells are ringing!**

Group 1: **Morning bells are ringing!**

All: **Ding, ding, dong!**
Ding, ding, dong!

Write a new song that tells Brother John
it is time to go to bed.

Today Is Monday

A Traditional Rhyme from England

✳✳

Group 1: **Today is Monday,**
Today is Monday,
Monday wash day.

All: **All you hungry brothers,**
We wish the same to you.

Group 2: **Today is Tuesday,**
Today is Tuesday,
Tuesday string beans,
Monday wash day.

All: **All you hungry brothers,**
We wish the same to you.

Go on to the next page.

Today Is Monday, p. 2

A Traditional Rhyme from England

****

Group 1: **Today is Wednesday,**
Today is Wednesday,
Wednesday soup,
Tuesday string beans,
Monday wash day.

All: **All you hungry brothers,**
We wish the same to you.

Group 2: **Today is Thursday,**
Today is Thursday,
Thursday roast beef,
Wednesday soup,
Tuesday string beans,
Monday wash day.

All: **All you hungry brothers,**
We wish the same to you.

Continue the rhyme for the other
days of the week: Friday—fish;
Saturday—payday; Sunday—rest day.

Thanksgiving Day

Lydia Maria Child

✳✳

Group 1: Over the river and through the wood,
To Grandfather's house we go;
The horse knows the way
To carry the sleigh
Through the white and drifted snow.

Group 2: Over the river and through the wood—
Oh, how the wind does blow!
It stings the toes and bites the nose,
As over the ground we go.

Group 1: Over the river and through the wood
Trot fast, my dapple-gray!
Spring over the ground
Like a hunting hound!
For this is Thanksgiving Day.

Go on to the next page.

Choral Reading 2-3, SV 1312-9

Thanksgiving Day, p. 2

Lydia Maria Child

****

Group 2:   Over the river and through the wood,
           And straight through the barnyard gate.
           We seem to go extremely slow—
           It is so hard to wait!

All: Over the river and through the wood—
           Now Grandmother's cap I spy!
           Hurray for the fun!

Solo 1:   Is the pudding done?

All: Hurray for the pumpkin pie!

Draw a picture of a
Thanksgiving celebration.

I Saw Three Ships

Author Unknown

✳✳

All: I saw three ships come sailing by,
Come sailing by, come sailing by,
I saw three ships come sailing by,
On New Year's Day in the morning.

And what do you think was in them then,
Was in them then, was in them then?
And what do you think was in them then,
On New Year's Day in the morning?

Go on to the next page.

Name _____ Date _____

I Saw Three Ships, p. 2

Author Unknown

✱✱

Girls: **Three pretty girls were in them then,**
Were in them then, were in them then,
Three pretty girls were in them then,
On New Year's Day in the morning.

Boys: **One could whistle, and one could sing,**
And one could play the violin;
Such joy there was at my wedding,
On New Year's Day in the morning.

Make a list of the special events and celebrations you want to attend in the new year.

We Shall Overcome

Adapted Spiritual

✳✳

All: We shall overcome,
We shall overcome,
We shall overcome someday.
Oh, here in my heart
I do believe
We shall overcome someday.

Group 1:   We shall build a new world,
We shall build a new world,
We shall build a new world someday.
Oh, here in my heart
I do believe
We shall build a new world someday.

Go on to the next page.

We Shall Overcome, p. 2

Adapted Spiritual

✳✳

Group 2:   We shall walk in peace,
We shall walk in peace,
We shall walk in peace someday.
Oh, here in my heart
I do believe
We shall walk in peace someday.

All: We shall overcome,
We shall overcome,
We shall overcome someday.
Oh, here in my heart
I do believe
We shall overcome someday.

 Read some of Dr. Martin Luther King's speeches.

Name _____ Date _____

Happy Valentine's Day

Melissa Blackwell Burke

✳✳✳✳✳✳✳✳✳✳✳✳✳✳✳✳✳✳✳✳✳✳✳✳✳✳✳✳✳✳✳✳✳✳✳✳✳✳

All: **Valentine's Day is a good time to say**
How we feel about friends
Who are near or far away.

Group 1:   **For friends who speak French:**
Je vous aime (juh voo zem)
I love you. Oh, yes I do.

Group 2:   **For friends who speak Spanish:**
Yo te amo (yoe teh ah-moe)
I love you. Oh, yes I do.

Go on to the next page.

Name _____ Date _____

Happy Valentine's Day, p. 2

Melissa Blackwell Burke

✳✳

Group 3: **For friends who speak German:**
Ich liebe dich (eesh lee-bah deesh)
I love you. Oh, yes I do.

All: **Valentine's Day is a good time to say**
How we feel about friends
Who are near or far away.

Make a Valentine card. Write "I love you" in one of the other languages from the rhyme.

Name _____   Date _____

Washington and Lincoln

Melissa Blackwell Burke

****

All: **On President's Day**
                   We recall
                   Two Presidents who helped one and all.

Group 1:   **He cut down a cherry tree.**
                   He couldn't tell a lie.

Group 2:   **He was born in a log cabin.**
                   He read by candlelight.

Group 1:   **He helped win our freedom from the king.**
                   He led us to build a new country.

Group 2:   **He wanted all people to be free.**
                   He made our country better for you and me.

Go on to the next page.

Choral Reading 2-3, SV 1312-9

Name _____ Date _____

Washington and Lincoln, p. 2

Melissa Blackwell Burke

✴✴✴✴✴✴✴✴✴✴✴✴✴✴✴✴✴✴✴✴✴✴✴✴✴✴✴✴✴✴✴✴✴✴✴✴✴

All: Who are the Presidents we spoke of before?
            Do you know? Are you sure?

Group 1:   George Washington!

Group 2:   Abraham Lincoln!

All: These are two great men
            our country claims.
            Without them,
            America would not be the same.

Read more about Washington and
Lincoln. Then pretend to be one of them.
Have a friend interview you about what
you did as President.

Michael Finnegan

Irish Naming Rhyme

****

Group 1: There was a man named Michael Finnegan.
He had whiskers on his chin-again.
They fell out and then grew in again.
Poor old Michael Finnegan.

Solo 1: Begin again!

Group 2: There was a man named Michael Finnegan.
He went fishing with a pin-again.
Caught a fish and dropped it in again.
Poor old Michael Finnegan.

Solo 1: Begin again!

Go on to the next page.

Name _____ Date _____

Michael Finnegan, p. 2

Irish Naming Rhyme

✳✳✳

All: There was a man named Michael Finnegan.
            He grew fat and then grew thin again.
            Then he died and had to begin again.
            Poor old Michael Finnegan.

Solo 2:   **Cut!**

 Make a collage of all green pictures
to represent the luck o' the Irish on
St. Patrick's Day.

Chinese New Year

Melissa Blackwell Burke

✳✳✳

Solo 1: **In China, there's a legend
about the monster Nian.**

All: **At the end of the year
Nian monster is near—
We must frighten Nian away!**

Solo 2: **If it's Nian you fear,
Then just listen here,
For three things
Will keep Nian away.**

Group 1: **Nian does not like loud noise.
That's why girls and boys
Pop fireworks to keep Nian away.**

Go on to the next page.

Chinese New Year, p. 2

Melissa Blackwell Burke

✳✳✳

Group 2:   Nian does not like it bright,
           So candles and fires we light
           To shine and keep Nian away.

Group 3:   Nian does not like to see red,
           So we paint our doors red
           To say, "Nian, you keep away!"

All: Remember these three
           And Nian will flee!

Read more about Chinese
New Year customs.

Name _____ Date _____

If All the World Were Paper
Adapted Traditional

✳✳

Group 1:   **If all the world were paper,**

Group 2:   **If all the world were paper,**

Group 1:   **And all the sea were ink,**

Group 2:   **And all the sea were ink,**

Group 1:   **If all the trees were bread and cheese,**

Group 2:   **If all the trees were bread and cheese,**

All: **What should we have to drink?**

Go on to the next page.

If All the World Were Paper, p. 2

Adapted Traditional

****

Group 2:   If all the world were sand,
Oh, then what should we lack?
If on the way there were no clay,
How would we get there and back?

Group 1:   If all things were eternal,
And nothing their end bringing,
If this should be, then how should we,
Here make an end of singing?

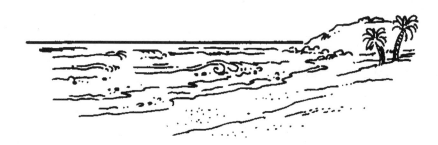

Write a new verse to continue this rhyme.
Begin with "If all the world were _____."

Two Silly Ladies

Traditional Folk Rhymes

✳✳

All: **Anna Elise, she jumped with surprise.**

Group 1:   **The surprise was so quick,**

Group 2:   **It played her a trick.**

Group 1:   **The trick was so rare,**

Group 2:   **She jumped a chair.**

Group 1:   **The chair was so frail,**

Group 2:   **She jumped in a pail.**

Group 1:   **The pail was so wet,**

Group 2:   **She jumped in a net.**

Group 1:   **The net was so small,**

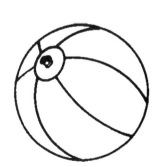

Group 2:   **She jumped on a ball.**

All: **The ball was so round,**
           She jumped on the ground.
           And ever since then
           She's been turning around!

Go on to the next page.

Choral Reading 2-3, SV 1312-9

Name _____   Date _____

Two Silly Ladies, p. 2

Traditional Folk Rhymes

****

All: I went downtown
            to see Mrs. Brown.
            She gave me a nickel
            To buy a pickle.

Group 2:   The pickle was sour,

Group 1:   She gave me a flower.

Group 2:   The flower was dead,

Group 1:   She gave me a thread.

Group 2:   The thread was thin,

Group 1:   She gave me a pin.

Group 2:   The pin was sharp,

Group 1:   She gave me a harp.

All: And the harp began to sing,
            "Minnie and a Minnie, and a ha, ha, ha!"

 Make up even more silly stories by adding to the rhyme. For example, "The pickle was so sour that _____."

Name _____ Date _____

Calico Pie

Edward Lear

✳✳✳✳✳✳✳✳✳✳✳✳✳✳✳✳✳✳✳✳✳✳✳✳✳✳✳✳✳✳✳✳✳✳✳✳✳✳

Group 1: **Calico Pie,**
The little Birds fly
Down to the Calico Tree.
Their wings were blue,
And they sang "Tilly-loo!"
Till away they flew—

All: **And they never came back to me!**
They never came back!
They never came back!
They never came back to me!

Go on to the next page.

Choral Reading 2-3, SV 1312-9

Calico Pie, p. 2

Edward Lear

✳✳

Group 2: **Calico Drum,**
The Grasshoppers come,
The Butterfly, Beetle, and Bee,
Over the ground,
Around and round,
With a hop and a bound—

All: **And they never came back to me!**
They never came back!
They never came back!
They never came back to me!

Write a few lines asking the birds
or insects to come back.

Have You Ever Seen?

Anonymous

✳✳

Group 1:   **Have you ever seen a sheet on a riverbed?**

Group 2:   **Or a single hair from a hammer's head?**

Group 3:   **Has the foot of a mountain any toes?**

All: **And is there a pair of garden hose?**

Group 1:   **Does the needle ever wink its eye?**

Group 2:   **Why doesn't the wing of a building fly?**

All: **Or open a trunk of a tree at all?**

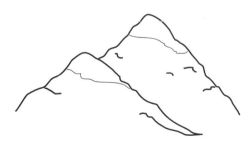

Go on to the next page.

Choral Reading 2-3, SV 1312-9

Name _____   Date _____

Have You Ever Seen?, p. 2

Anonymous

****

Group 1:   **Are the teeth of a rake ever going to bite?**

Group 2:   **Have the hands of a clock any left or right?**

Group 3:   **Can the garden plot be deep and dark?**

All: **And what is the sound of the birch's bark?**

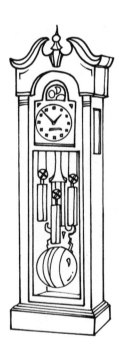

Draw a picture of something described in one of the lines. For example, you might draw a needle winking its eye.

Name _____ Date _____

Betty Botter

✳✳

All: **Betty Botter bought some butter,
            But, she said,**

Group 1:   **"The butter's bitter.**

Group 2:   **If I put it in my batter**

Group 1:   **It will make my batter bitter.**

Group 2:   **But a bit of better butter—**

Group 1:   **That would make my batter better."**

Go on to the next page.

     Choral Reading 2-3, SV 1312-9

Betty Botter, p. 2

✳✳✳✳✳✳✳✳✳✳✳✳✳✳✳✳✳✳✳✳✳✳✳✳✳✳✳✳✳✳✳✳✳✳✳✳✳

All: **So she bought a bit of butter,**
Better than her bitter butter.

Group 2: **And she put it in her batter,**

Group 1: **And the batter was not bitter.**

All: **So 'twas better Betty Botter**
Bought a bit of better butter.

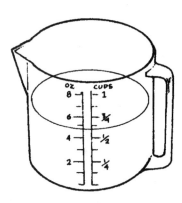

Take turns with a partner saying other
tongue twisters you know.

Weather Medley

✳✳

Solo 1:   **Whether the weather be fine,**

Solo 2:   **Or whether the weather be not,**

Both: **We'll weather the weather**
            whatever the weather
            whether we like it or not!

All: **Showery, Flowery!**

Solo 3:   **The wind, the wind,**

Solo 4:   **The wind blew high,**

Both: **The rain comes falling from the sky!**

All: **Showery, Flowery!**

Go on to the next page.

Weather Medley, p. 2

✳✳

Solo 5: **The rain is raining all around,**

Solo 6: **It falls on field and tree,**

Both: **It rains on the umbrellas here,**
      And on the ships at sea!

All: **Showery, Flowery!**

Solo 7: **Ring around the Moon,**

Solo 8: **Rain is coming soon!**

All: **Showery, Flowery!**

Pretend to give a weather report that predicts rain.

A Calendar

Sara Coleridge

Group 1:   **January brings the snow,**
          Makes our feet and fingers glow.

Group 2:   **February brings the rain,**
          Thaws the frozen lake again.

Group 3:   **March brings breezes, loud and shrill,**
          To stir the dancing daffodil.

Group 1:   **April brings the primrose sweet,**
          Scatters daisies at our feet.

Group 2:   **May brings flocks of pretty lambs**
          Skipping by their fleecy dams.

Group 3:   **June brings tulips, lilies, roses,**
          Fills the children's hands with posies.

Group 1:   **Hot July brings cooling showers,**
          Apricots, and gillyflowers.

Go on to the next page.

A Calendar, p. 2

Sara Coleridge

✳✳✳

Group 2: **August brings the sheaves of corn,**
Then the harvest home is borne.

Group 3: **Warm September brings the fruit;**
Sportsmen then begin to shoot.

Group 1: **Fresh October brings the pheasant;**
Then to gather nuts is pleasant.

Group 2: **Dull November brings the blahs;**
Then the leaves are whirling fast.

Group 3: **Chill December brings the sleet,**
Blazing fire, and Christmas treat.

Write a rhyme about the month
in which you were born.

46

Choral Reading 2-3, SV 1312-9

Name _____ Date _____

The Wind

Robert Louis Stevenson

✳✳

Group 1: I saw you toss the kites on high
And blow the birds about the sky;
And all around I heard you pass,
Like ladies' skirts across the grass—

All: O wind, a-blowing all day long,
O wind, that sings so loud a song!

Group 2: I saw the different things you did,
But always you yourself you hid.
I felt you push, I heard you call,
I could not see yourself at all—

All: O wind, a-blowing all day long,
O wind, that sings so loud a song!

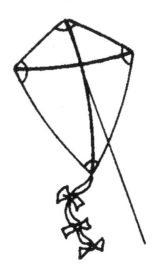

Go on to the next page.

Choral Reading 2-3, SV 1312-9

The Wind, p. 2

Robert Louis Stevenson

****

All:

O you that are so strong and cold,
O blower, are you young or old?
Are you a beast of field and tree,
Or just a stronger child than me?

Solo 1:

O wind, a-blowing all day long,
O wind, that sings so loud a song!

How would the world be different
if there were no wind? Talk about
it with a partner.

Autumn Fires

Robert Louis Stevenson

****

Group 1:   **In the other gardens**
            And all up the vale,
            From the autumn bonfires

All: **See the smoke trail!**

Group 2:   **Pleasant summer over**
            And all the summer flowers,
            The red fire blazes,

All: **The gray smoke towers.**

Go on to the next page.

       Choral Reading 2-3, SV 1312-9

Name _____ Date _____

Autumn Fires, p. 2

Robert Louis Stevenson

❋❋

Group 3: **Sing a song of seasons!**
Something bright in all!
Flowers in the summer,

All: **Fires in the fall!**

Make a Venn diagram that
compares summer to fall.

50   Choral Reading 2-3, SV 1312-9

Snowy Day

Author Unknown

✳✳

Group 1: **This is how snowflakes play about;**
Up in cloudland they dance in and out.
(Wiggle fingers above head.)

Group 2: **This is how they whirl down the street,**
Powdering everybody they meet.
(Wiggle fingers and move hands left to right.)

Group 3: **This is how snowflakes cover the tree;**
Each branch and twig bends in the breeze.
(Move hands down and inward.)

Group 1: **This is how snowflakes blow in a heap,**
Looking just like fleecy sheep.
(Move hands over each other repeatedly.)

Go on to the next page.

Snowy Day, p. 2

Author Unknown

✳✳✳✳✳✳✳✳✳✳✳✳✳✳✳✳✳✳✳✳✳✳✳✳✳✳✳✳✳✳✳✳✳✳✳✳✳✳✳

Group 2:   **This is how they cover the ground,**
            Cover it thickly, with never a sound.
            (Hold fingers to lips.)

Group 3:   **This is how people shiver and shake**
            On a snowy morning when first they wake.
            (Pretend to shiver and shake.)

All: **This is how snowflakes melt away**
            When the Sun sends out its beams to play.
            (Move hands around back.)

Cut a snowflake shape from white paper.
Write a short rhyme about snow.

The Green Grass Grew All Around

Traditional

✱✱

Group 1: **There was a tree,**

Group 2: **There was a tree,**

Group 1: **The prettiest tree**

Group 2: **The prettiest tree**

Group 1: **That you ever did see.**

Group 2: **That you ever did see.**

All: **The tree in a hole,**
          and the hole in the ground,
          And the green grass grew
          All around and around.
          And the green grass grew all around!

Go on to the next page.

The Green Grass Grew All Around, p. 2

Traditional

✳✳

Group 1:   **And on that tree**

Group 2:   **And on that tree**

Group 1:   **There was a limb,**

Group 2:   **There was a limb,**

Group 1:   **The prettiest limb**

Group 2:   **The prettiest limb**

Group 1:   **That you ever did see.**

Group 2:   **That you ever did see.**

All: **The limb on the tree,**
           and the tree in the hole,
           And the green grass grew
           All around and around.
           And the green grass grew all around!

Go on to the next page.

The Green Grass Grew All Around, p. 3

Traditional

✲✲

Group 1: And on that limb, there was a branch,
The prettiest branch
That you ever did see.

All: The branch on the limb,
And the limb on the tree,
And the tree in the hole,
And the green grass grew
All around and around.
The green grass grew all around!

Group 2: And on that branch, there was a nest,
The prettiest nest
That you ever did see.

All: The nest on the branch,
And the branch on the limb,
And the limb on the tree,
And the tree in the hole,
And the green grass grew
All around and around.
The green grass grew all around!

Trees help Earth in many ways.
Plant a tree!

Over in the Meadow

Traditional

****

All: Over in the meadow in the sand in the Sun
             Lived an old mother turtle and her little turtle one.

Solo 1:   "Dig!" said the mother. "I dig!" said the one.

All: So they dug all day in the sand in the Sun.

All: Over in the meadow where the stream runs blue,
             Lived an old mother fish and her little fishies two.

Solo 2:   "Swim!" said the mother. "We swim!" said the two.

All: So they swam all day where the stream runs blue.

All: Over in the meadow in a hole in a tree,
             Lived a mother bluebird and her little birdies three.

Solo 3:   "Sing!" said the mother. "We sing!" said the three.

All: So they sang all day in the hole in the tree.

Go on to the next page.

                                       Choral Reading 2-3, SV 1312-9

Name _____ Date _____

Over in the Meadow, p. 2

Traditional

✳✳

All: Over in the meadow by the reeds by the shore
                    Lived a mother muskrat and her little ratties four.
Solo 4:   "Dive!" said the mother. "We dive!" said the four.
All: So they dove all day in the reeds by the shore.

All: Over in the meadow in a snug beehive
                    Lived a mother honeybee and her little honeys five.
Solo 5:   "Buzz!" said the mother. "We buzz!" said the five.
All: So they buzzed all day in the snug beehive.

All: Over in the meadow in a nest built of sticks
                    Lived an old mother crow and her little crows six.
Solo 6:   "Caw!" said the mother. "We caw!" said the six.
All: So they cawed all day in their nest built of sticks.

All: Over in the meadow in the grass nice and even
                    Lived a mother cricket and her little crickets seven.
Solo 7:   "Chirp!" said the mother. "We chirp!" said the seven.
All: So they chirped all day in the grass nice and even.

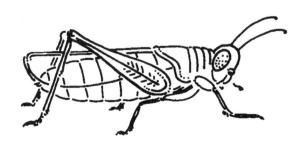

Go on to the next page.

Over in the Meadow, p. 3

Traditional

✳✳✳✳✳✳✳✳✳✳✳✳✳✳✳✳✳✳✳✳✳✳✳✳✳✳✳✳✳✳✳✳✳✳✳✳✳✳✳

All: **Over in the meadow by the old mossy gate**
            Lived a mother lizard and her little lizards eight.
Solo 8:   **"Bask!" said the mother. "We bask!" said the eight.**
All: **So they basked all day by the old mossy gate.**

All: **Over in the meadow where the clear pools shine**
            Lived an old mother frog and her little froggies nine.
Solo 9:   **"Jump!" said the mother. "We jump!" said the nine.**
All: **So they jumped all day where the clear pools shine.**

All: **Over in the meadow in a cozy wee den**
            Lived an old mother beaver
            and her little beavers ten.
Solo 10:   **"Beave!" said the mother. "We beave!" said the ten.**
All: **So they beaved all day in a cozy wee den.**

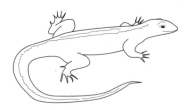

With a group, paint a mural of the
meadow scene.

Animal Fair

Traditional

✳✳

Group 1:   **We went to the animal fair.**

Group 2:   **The birds and the beasts were there.**

Group 1:   **The big baboon by the light of the Moon**

Group 2:   **Was combing his auburn hair.**

Group 1:   **You should have seen the monk;**

Group 2:   **He sat on the elephant's trunk;**

Group 1:   **The elephant sneezed and fell on his knees,**

Group 2:   **And what became of the monk,**

All: **The monk, the monk, the monk?**

Go on to the next page.

Animal Fair, p. 2

Traditional

****

Group 1: (Say **the monk, the monk** repeatedly while
Group 2 reads.)

Group 2: **We went to the animal fair.**
The birds and the beasts were there.
The big baboon by the light of the Moon
Was combing his auburn hair.

Group 2: (Say **the monk, the monk** repeatedly while
Group 1 reads.)

Group 1: **You should have seen the monk;**
He sat on the elephant's trunk;
The elephant sneezed and fell on his knees,

All: **And what became of the monk,**
The monk, the monk, the monk?

Make paper plate masks of the baboon,
the elephant, and the monkey.

The Leopard

Lord Alfred Douglas

✳✳✳

All:

The leopard always seems to feel
That he is ready for a meal,

Group 1:

Although he mostly comes by night
To satisfy his appetite.

Group 2:

And you will quickly guess, I think,
The things he likes to eat and drink.

Go on to the next page.

The Leopard, p. 2

Lord Alfred Douglas

✳✳✳✳✳✳✳✳✳✳✳✳✳✳✳✳✳✳✳✳✳✳✳✳✳✳✳✳✳✳✳✳✳✳✳✳✳✳

Group 1:   **He really is a dreadful trial;**
           He never takes the least denial.

Group 2:   **And if you're out when he should call,**
           He waits for hours in the hall.

All: **He is a very hungry beast**
           And always ready for a feast.

Move around the room like a leopard as you listen to a partner read the poem.

Choral Reading 2-3, SV 1312-9

The Squirrel

Anonymous

✳✳✳

Group 1: **Whisky, frisky,**
Hippity hop,
Up he goes
To the treetop!

Group 2: **Whirly, twirly,**
Round and round,
Down he scampers
To the ground.

Go on to the next page.

The Squirrel, p. 2

Anonymous

✳✳

Group 3: **Furly, curly,**
What a tail!
Tall as a feather,
Broad as a sail!

All: **Where's his supper?**
In the shell—
Snappity, crackity,
Out it fell!

Make a menu for a pretend restaurant
for squirrels.

Name _____ Date _____

Skylark

Christina Rossetti

✳✳✳

Group 1:   **The Earth was green, the sky was blue:**
I saw and heard one sunny morn
A skylark hang between the two,
A singing speck above the corn;

Group 2:   **A stage below, in gay accord,**
White butterflies danced on the wing,
And still the singing skylark soared,
And silent sank, and soared to sing.

Go on to the next page.

Name _____   Date _____

Skylark, p. 2

Christina Rossetti

****

Group 3:   The cornfield stretched a tender green
              To right and left beside my walks;
              I knew he had a nest unseen
              Somewhere among the million stalks.

All: And as I paused to hear his song,
              While swift the sunny moments slid,
              Perhaps his mate sat listening long,
              And listened longer than I did.

 Use an envelope to make a bird puppet.
Put your hand in the envelope to make
the beak move. Draw details. Tape a
body to the envelope.

What Is Pink?

Christina Rossetti

****

Group 1:   **What is pink?**

Group 2:   **A rose is pink**
by the fountain's brink.
What is red?

Group 1:   **A poppy's red in its barley bed.**
What is blue?

Group 2:   **The sky is blue**
where the clouds float through.
What is white?

Group 1:   **A swan is white sailing in the light.**
What is yellow?

Go on to the next page.

Name _____ Date _____

What Is Pink?, p. 2
Christina Rossetti

****

Group 2: **Pears are yellow,**
rich and ripe and mellow.
What is green?

Group 1: **The grass is green**
with small flowers in between.
What is violet?

Group 2: **Clouds are violet**
in the summer twilight.
What is orange?

All: **Why, an orange,**
Just an orange!

Make a collage with objects
of all one color.

Name _____ Date _____

If

Author Unknown

****

Group 1: **If all the seas were one sea,**
What a great sea that would be!

Group 2: **If all the trees were one tree,**
What a great tree that would be!

Group 1: **If all the axes were one ax,**
What a great ax that would be!

Group 2: **And if all the men were one man,**
What a great man that would be!

Go on to the next page.

If, p. 2
Author Unknown

✳✳✳

Group 1: **And if the great man took the great ax,
And cut down the great tree,**

Group 2: **And let if fall into the great sea,**

All: **What a splish-splash that would be!**

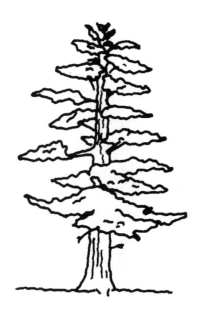

Work with a partner. Write a new version of this poem by describing other things, such as *If all the boats were one boat.*

The Star

Jane Taylor

✳✳

All:
Twinkle, twinkle, little star,
How I wonder what you are!
Up above the world so high,
Like a diamond in the sky.

Group 1:
When the blazing Sun is gone,
When it nothing shines upon,
Then you show your little light,
Twinkle, twinkle, all the night.

Group 2:
Then the traveller in the dark,
Thanks you for your tiny spark;
He could not see which way to go,
If you did not twinkle so.

Go on to the next page.

Name _____   Date _____

The Star, p. 2

Jane Taylor

✳✳✳

Group 1:   **In the dark blue sky you keep,**
And often through my curtains peep,

Group 2:   **For you never shut your eye,**
Till the Sun is in the sky.

All: **As your bright and tiny spark**
Lights the traveller in the dark—
Though I know not what you are,
Twinkle, twinkle, little star.

Put a piece of crumpled foil under a clear bowl of water. Turn off the lights. Tap the top of the water. Shine a flashlight. Look into the bowl. Look up at the ceiling for starshine.

Choral Reading 2-3, SV 1312-9

The Land of Nod

Robert Louis Stevenson

****

Group 1:   **From breakfast on through all the day**
At home among my friends I stay,
But every night I go abroad
Afar into the land of Nod.

Group 2:   **All by myself I have to go,**
With none to tell me what to do—
All alone beside the streams
And up the mountainsides of dreams.

Go on to the next page.

The Land of Nod, p. 2

Robert Louis Stevenson

✱✱

Group 3:   **The strangest things are there for me,**
Both things to eat and things to see,
And many frightening sights abroad
Till morning in the land of Nod.

All: **Try as I like to find the way,**
I never can get back by day,
Nor can remember plain and clear
The curious music that I hear.

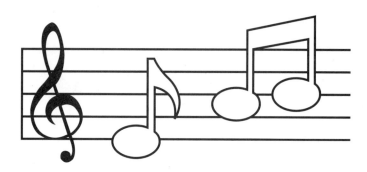

Draw a picture of yourself having
an interesting dream.

Choral Reading 2-3, SV 1312-9

My Shadow

Robert Louis Stevenson

****

All: **I have a little shadow**
       that goes in and out with me.
       And what can be the use of him
       Is more than I can see.

Group 1:   **He is very, very like me**
          from the heels up to the head,
          And I see him jump before me
          when I jump into my bed.

Group 2:   **The funniest thing about him**
          is the way he likes to grow—
          Not at all like proper children,
          which is always very slow,

Go on to the next page.

Choral Reading 2-3, SV 1312-9

My Shadow, p. 2

Robert Louis Stevenson

****

Group 3:   For he sometimes shoots up taller
Like an india-rubber ball,
And he sometimes gets so little
that there's none of him at all.

All: One morning, very early,
before the Sun was up,
I rose and found the shining dew
on every buttercup;
But my lazy little shadow,
like an arrant sleepy-head,
Had stayed at home behind me
And was fast asleep in bed.

Take turns with a partner holding
a flashlight. Make shadow shapes
on a wall.

     Choral Reading 2-3, SV 1312-9

The Swing

Robert Louis Stevenson

****

All: How do you like to go up in a swing,
Up in the air so blue?
Oh, I do think it the pleasantest thing
Ever a child can do!

Group 1:   Up in the air and over the wall,
Till I can see so wide,
Rivers and trees and cattle and all
Over the countryside—

Go on to the next page.

The Swing, p. 2

Robert Louis Stevenson

****

Group 2: **Till I look down on the garden green**
Down on the roof so brown—
Up in the air I go flying again,
Up in the air and down!

All: **How do you like to go up in a swing,**
Up in the air so blue?
Oh, I do think it the pleasantest thing
Ever a child can do!

Memorize one of the stanzas of this poem. Say it with a partner as you swing on the playground.

Turtle Soup

Lewis Carroll

✳✳

Group 1:   **Beautiful Soup, so rich and green,**
Waiting in a hot tureen!
Who for such dainties would not stoop?
Soup of the evening, beautiful Soup!
Soup of the evening, beautiful Soup!

All: **Beau—ootiful Soo—oop!**
Beau—ootiful Soo—oop!
Soo—oop of the e—e—evening,
Beautiful, beautiful Soup!

Go on to the next page.

79

Turtle Soup, p. 2

Lewis Carroll

****

Group 2: **Beautiful Soup! Who cares for fish,**
Game, or any other dish?
Who would not give all else for two
Pennyworth only of beautiful Soup?
Pennyworth only of beautiful Soup?

All: **Beau—ootiful Soo—oop!**
Beau—ootiful Soo—oop!
Soo—oop of the e—evening,
Beautiful, beauti—FUL SOUP!

Write a recipe for your favorite real or silly soup.

80 Choral Reading 2-3, SV 1312-9

Ravioli
Traditional

✳✳✳

All: **Ravioli, ravioli—**
Ravioli, that's the stuff for me.

Group 1: **Do you have it on your sleeve?**
Group 2: **Yes, I have it on my sleeve.**
Group 1: **On your sleeve?**
Group 2: **On my sleeve.**

All: **Ravioli, ravioli—**
Ravioli, that's the stuff for me.

Group 1: **Do you have it on your pants?**
Group 2: **Yes, I have I have it on my pants.**
Group 1: **On your pants?**
Group 2: **On my pants.**

Go on to the next page.

Ravioli, p. 2

Traditional

❊❊❊❊❊❊❊❊❊❊❊❊❊❊❊❊❊❊❊❊❊❊❊❊❊❊❊❊❊❊❊❊❊❊❊❊❊❊❊

All: **Ravioli, ravioli—**
            Ravioli, that's the stuff for me.

Group 1:   **Do you have it on your shoe?**
Group 2:   **Yes, I have it on my shoe.**
Group 1:   **On your shoe?**
Group 2:   **On my shoe.**
Group 1:   **On your pants?**
Group 2:   **On my pants.**
Group 1:   **On your seleve?**
Group 2:   **On my sleeve.**

All: **Ravioli, ravioli—**
            Ravioli, that's the stuff for me!

Sing this poem to the tune of "Alouette."

Name _____ Date _____

Manners Medley

Robert Louis Stevenson and Unknown Authors

✳✳

Solo 1:   **When it is time to speak or dine,**
Here are some things to keep in mind:

Group 1:   **A child should always say what's true,**

Group 2:   **And speak when he is spoken to,**

Group 3:   **And behave mannerly at the table;**

All: **At least as far as he is able.**

Go on to the next page.

Manners Medley, p. 2

Robert Louis Stevenson and Unknown Authors

****

Solo 2: And, if by chance, some friends you meet
As you are walking down the street—
Here is a way to greet them.

Group 1: One misty, moisty morning,
When cloudy was the weather,

Group 2: I chanced to meet an old man,
Clothed all in leather.

Group 3: He began to compliment
And I began to grin.

All: How do you do?
And how do you do?
And how do you do again?

Write a new verse about a way to show good manners, such as sharing with a friend.

Choral Reading 2-3, SV 1312-9

Hurt No Living Thing

Adapted

Original by Christina Rossetti

✳✳

All: **Hurt no living thing:**

Group 1:   **Ladybug or butterfly,**

All: **Hurt no living thing:**

Group 2:   **Nor moth with dusty wing,**

All: **Hurt no living thing:**

Group 1:   **Nor cricket chirping cheerily,**

All: **Hurt no living thing:**

Go on to the next page.

Hurt No Living Thing, p. 2

Adapted

Original by Christina Rossetti

❋❋❋

Group 2:   **Nor grasshopper so light of leap,**

All: **Hurt no living thing:**

Group 1:   **Nor dancing gnat, nor beetle fat,**

All: **Hurt no living thing:**

Group 2:   **Nor harmless worms that creep.**

Solo 1:   **Please, hurt no living thing!**

Name _____ Date _____

The Gingerbread Man
Traditional

✳✳✳

Group 1: **Once upon a time,
a little old woman baked a gingerbread man.
She baked it just for her grandchildren.
Just as she opened the oven, the gingerbread
man jumped off the pan and ran out the door.**

All: **The gingerbread man said,
"Run, run, as fast as you can!
You can't catch me—
I'm the gingerbread man!"**

Group 2: **A horse tried to catch the gingerbread man.
It couldn't.
A cow tried to catch the gingerbread man.
It couldn't.
A cat tried to catch the gingerbread man.
It couldn't.
A dog tried to catch the gingerbread man.
It couldn't.**

Go on to the next page.

The Gingerbread Man, p. 2
Traditional

❋❋❋❋❋❋❋❋❋❋❋❋❋❋❋❋❋❋❋❋❋❋❋❋❋❋❋❋❋❋❋❋❋❋❋❋❋❋❋

Group 1:   **The gingerbread man ran on and on.**

All: **"Run, run, as fast as you can.**
You can't catch me—
I'm the gingerbread man!"

Group 2:   **Even a fox**
could not catch the gingerbread man.
Then he came upon two children.
They were the old woman's grandchildren.
"I'll let them catch me," said the gingerbread man.
"After all, these are the children I was baked for."

Solo 1:   **This was the best fate that could befall the**
gingerbread man, don't you think?

Name _____ Date _____

Clever Girl

A Jewish Folktale

✳✳✳✳✳✳✳✳✳✳✳✳✳✳✳✳✳✳✳✳✳✳✳✳✳✳✳✳✳✳✳✳✳✳✳✳✳✳

Group 1: Once upon a time,
a poor farmer needed to pay a tax.
The king went to the farmer's home.
He asked for the money.
The farmer had none. But he had a smart daughter.
"I will have to ask my daughter what to do," said
the farmer.

Group 2: "Is she really so smart?" asked the king.
"If so, tell her to empty the sea with this tiny cup.
I will be back in a week."

Group 1: The next week, the king went back.
"I will empty the sea with this cup," said the girl.
"I will do it when you stop all the rivers with
this stone."
The king laughed. "You are a very clever girl.
Would you be my wife?"

Go on to the next page.

Clever Girl, p. 2

A Jewish Folktale

✳✳✳

Group 2: **The girl said she would.**
But the king must give her one wish.
"If you ever ask me to leave, I may take one
thing with me."

Group 1: **Years went by.**
The kingdom fared well.
The king and the queen were happy.

Group 2: **But one day, the king became angry.**
He asked the queen to leave.
"Be gone tomorrow," said the king.
"I remember my promise.
You may take your favorite thing with you."

Group 1: **When the king woke up the next morning,**
he was not in his palace.
He was traveling with the queen.
"You said I could take my favorite thing," she said.
The king and queen laughed.

Write about your favorite thing.
Tell why you like it so.

Choral Reading 2-3, SV 1312-9

Belling the Cat

An Aesop Fable

****

All: **Once upon a time,**
the mice had a big problem—the cat.

Group 1: **The mice called a meeting.**
They spoke about their fear.
They felt something must be done.
If only they knew when the cat
was coming!

Group 2: **A young mouse stood up and said,**
"I have a simple plan that is sure to work.
All we have to do is hang a bell around
the cat's neck. When we hear the bell,
we will know the cat is near.

Go on to the next page.

Belling the Cat, p. 2

An Aesop Fable

****

Group 1: **All the mice were much surprised
that they had not thought of this before.
But in the midst of their celebration,
an old mouse rose and said,**

Group 2: **"The plan of the young mouse does
sound very good. But I have one question:
Who will bell the cat?"**

Solo 1: **It is one thing to say that something
should be done, but quite a different
matter to do it.**

Pretend you are the mice. Write a
"help wanted" poster for the job
of belling the cat.

King Midas

A Greek Tale

****

Group 1:   Long ago in Greece there lived
a king named Midas.
He had more gold than anyone,
but still he wanted more.

Group 1:   One day, as King Midas counted coins,
a stranger appeared.
"So much gold! So much gold!" he said.

Group 2:   "Not so much," said King Midas.
"I wish there were more.
In fact, I wish that everything I touched
would turn to gold."

Group 1:   "Then you shall have your wish,"
said the stranger. And he was gone.
King Midas rushed to the door.
When he touched it, it turned to gold.
King Midas was very happy.

Go on to the next page.

Name _____ Date _____

King Midas, p. 2

A Greek Tale

✳✳

Group 2: King Midas sat down to a feast to celebrate.
When he touched his cup, it turned to gold.
When he touched his bread, it turned to gold.
"Oh, no," said King Midas.
"I can't eat or drink gold."

Group 1: Just then, his daughter came in.
She ran to hug the king.
She turned to gold.
King Midas saw how foolish
his wish had been.

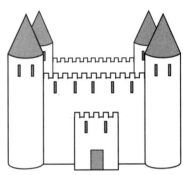

Group 2: The stranger came in.
When he saw King Midas knew
how foolish his wish had been,
he changed things back again.

Solo 1: Be careful what you wish for.
It just might come true!

Make a wish, but be careful!

Name _____ Date _____

The Crow and the Jug

An Aesop Fable

✳✳

All: The weather was very dry,
and the crow was thirsty indeed.

Group 1:   It happened that the crow came upon
a jug with a little bit of water in it.

Group 2:   But the jug was tall,
and it had a narrow neck.
No matter how hard he tried,
the crow could not reach the water.

Group 1:   The poor bird felt he might die of thirst.
Then an idea came to him!

Go on to the next page.

The Crow and the Jug, p. 2

An Aesop Fable

✳✳✳

Group 2:   **The crow picked up a tiny pebble.**
He dropped it into the jug.
The water rose a bit.

Group 1:   **One by one, the crow dropped in**
more pebbles.
And each time, the water rose a bit.

All: **Finally, it was near enough to the top**
that the crow could have a drink!

Solo 1:   **Use your head in times of trouble.**

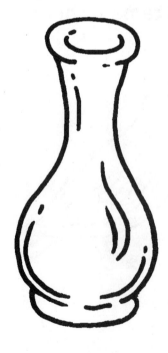